Job Security

BE THE LAST EMPLOYEE STANDING

Job Security

BE THE LAST EMPLOYEE STANDING

Michael Bradley

TWOHARBORS
WWW.TWOHARBORSPRESS.COM

Two Harbors Press
212 3rd Avenue North, Suite 290
Minneapolis, MN 55401
612.455.2293
www.TwoHarborsPress.com

ISBN-13: 978-1-938690-02-0
LCCN: 2012941703

Distributed by Itasca Books

Cover Design by Ryan Nygard
Typeset by Mary Nelson

Printed in the United States of America

This book is dedicated to my wife, Patricia, and my three daughters, Heather, Kristen, and Shannon

Table of Contents

Introduction

I recently retired from Bristol-Myers Squibb Co., Inc., a large pharmaceutical business, after thirty-seven years of service. Throughout that time, I held the same job, by choice, under a number of different supervisors. There were many changes in top management, with each new executive presenting a different slant on how to do the job.

My sales position required me to sell products to doctors and hospitals. I had to convince doctors to recommend my products to their patients. To accomplish this, I made as many friends in the office as possible, making it a point not to overlook anyone. You would be surprised who can help or hurt your success in any particular office. Knowing the benefits of my products over those of the competition was an absolute must. The bottom line was to find out what was important to the doctor, whether it be price, quality, availability, or all three. Once the doctor's needs were completely satisfied, I made the sale. The most difficult part of my job was keeping the business. This was where I excelled. I gave incredible service and took care of my doctors' every need. When they called, for whatever reason, it was important to them and that is what counted. I was available to take care of their every concern.

The hospital sale was much different. There were many people across several departments involved in the purchasing of any given product. I dealt with the chief of pediatrics, the obstetric and nursery supervisor, the purchasing department, administration (in some circumstances), the storeroom personnel, and the formulary committee. Every hospital is different; and at times influential people are found in unlikely places. You must know where they are to be successful. In most hospitals, the chief of pediatrics, the purchasing department, and the nursery supervisor are the key decision-makers. Other people are important and sometimes overlooked, but never by me. For example, someone in the storeroom can make your life miserable and derail the contract if they don't feel important to the process. It was essential for me to win over the person who ultimately made the decision. At the same time, I had to round up as many supporters as possible. Selling the product to everyone and explaining why it met his or her needs was a must. Many signed contracts are broken because a salesperson does not completely sell the product to all involved, so I always made sure that anyone involved in the handling and/or use of the product was convinced it was the best product available. In my years as a sales representative, I have never lost a signed contract.

Needless to say, to have a lasting career, you also have to be good at what you do. But whatever your job, whether it be in sales or an office, your ability to relate to people and make them feel important has a direct bearing on your success. To navigate such a maze of different philosophies and personalities, you must work well with people. For me, starting out with good people skills helped, but I learned so much more throughout my years on the job. Now, it's important to pass that knowledge on.

When you step into any new workplace, the learning process begins all over again. Chances are you will make many mistakes. I hope this book will help you think before you act. Much of what I mention comes from many years of work experience. You can't expect to have a wealth of experience when you walk into a new job. This is doubly true if you are changing industries or if you are new to the workforce.

Having information like this at the start of my career would have been of considerable help to me. I learned and used these principles throughout my tenure as a sales representative. There are no guarantees in this world, and sometimes our best efforts just don't work out. The information in this book will most definitely help secure your job.

Chapter 1

First Impressions

First impressions mean so much when looking for a new job. Dress appropriately when visiting a workplace office or conducting a professional meeting for the first time. You can't go wrong by dressing on the conservative side. Shave, comb your hair, press your shirt and pants, and stand up straight! Exude a contagious smile on your face. Greet everyone with a healthy handshake.

There are questions to think about and decisions to make before you even start to schedule interviews. Be sure to thoroughly check out the company online and know a great deal about the business before arriving for an interview.

The Interview

The interview will start with the employer asking you a number of questions. The best advice I can give anyone is to be completely truthful. If they ask a question such as, "Have you ever been fired from a job?" you must tell the truth and then explain why this happened. Many people are fired for the wrong reasons. An honest answer is always the best answer.

There is a mountain of information on the Internet about what questions to ask in an interview. Let me concentrate here on what not to ask. These are all bad questions to ask:

How much vacation would I get?
How many personal days and holidays are given?
What time can I leave at night?
How long are lunch and breaks?

Don't ask about pension plans or 401(k)s either. This information will be given once you are offered a job. Your sole purpose in this first interview is to convince the person conducting the interview that you are the right person for the job. Even if the give and take doesn't go as planned, act confident and tell the interviewer that you are the right person for the job.

So many people answer all the questions and just leave. The interviewer wants the applicant to show some initiative and ask to be hired. You can ask about how long the process takes should you be hired and when you can expect to hear something. Thank the interviewer for taking time out of his or her busy schedule to meet with you. Send a written note of thanks for the interview (not an email). Should you not hear anything in the allotted time, wait two more days and then call. Inform the hiring person that you are very interested in the position and are just following up to see if any additional information is needed.

When at the interview, take note of what people are wearing. Being a new employee, it is important to dress in the most conservative fashion for that particular work environment. If there are fifteen people in your work area and only two are wearing jeans, don't go there. You haven't earned the right to be different. Remember, you are the new kid who has to prove yourself. The same goes for shoes, hair, and overall appearance. Don't let any of these details define who you are (or are not). When you start work, some of your new colleagues will make rash judgments about you that could last for a long time.

Eventually the day will come when a person thinks enough of you and your ability to hire you for a position at XYZ Company. So now the job is yours and you are starting in two days. *Watch out world, here I come.*

Once you secure the job, it's time to plan for your success. The workplace can be nasty, and you must navigate through it very carefully in order to survive. Even though we live in a technological world, it is your people skills, or lack of them, that will determine how well you do.

Orientation

Use your good sense and ask about those items that directly impact your job. The company will probably give you a benefits book at orientation that covers those topics you don't want to ask about. One such topic is health insurance. If the company offers medical insurance, be sure to take a close look at the different options. One might have to pay more for better plans. Should you become seriously ill, this will be a valuable purchase. You should at least examine each plan closely and ask questions. The better informed you are, the easier it is to make the right choice for your situation.

If your company offers a 401(k) plan, join it. The company takes pretax money out of your pay and invests it for retirement. Some people think they are too young to worry about retirement and don't feel the need to save money. This is a big mistake. You won't miss money that you don't see, and these savings will grow over the next forty years. Some companies match a portion of the money you take out of your salary. Often, this means you can invest 6 percent or more into a 401(k), without paying taxes, until you retire. The company may contribute up to 3 percent. Should they do that, your savings grow up to 50 percent immediately.

If your company does not offer a 401(k) plan, you can open an individual retirement account (IRA) at any bank or brokerage house. This is another pretax option for investing your money. Another alternative is a Roth IRA, where after-tax money is invested. The advantage of this plan is that all of your gains are tax-free at retirement age.

During orientation, pay very close attention to what

you can't do as an employee. For legal reasons there are many items that could potentially be listed in this category. Most companies forbid personal use of work computers. They have guidelines for acceptable use, and you should adhere to them strictly. They have the right to check your company computer, cell phone, iPhone, Droid, BlackBerry, iPad, or anything else provided by them at any time.

Study and remember the company code of conduct. Other employees (maybe even direct supervisors) will tell you that some of this "stuff" is not important, but it is—always. The company committed the code to writing for a reason. This might not be a big deal to some people. Perhaps they haven't been caught violating the code of conduct or had the lack of compliance brought to their attention. Chances are that human resources (HR) and/or others have noticed and are keeping track of such individuals. When it comes time for an annual review and consideration for a pay raise, such employees may then hear of their noncompliance—as a reason to not receive a pay increase. My advice is to adhere strictly to the code at all times, regardless of what other employees do.

The company might want you to set up an online profile. This will introduce you to your new colleagues and give them some background information about you. Be very careful when drafting your profile. Don't include anything that might alienate coworkers. Hobbies like hunting are a negative for many people. If you are a member of an organization that may be construed by some as "extreme"—like PETA or the NRA or even the Freemasons—you might want to leave that out, too. Also, don't mention your religious or political party affiliations. This is your business and only yours.

People have very strong opinions about lifestyle choices and may make the wrong assumptions about you based on your pastime activities. So put in pastimes that are most likely not controversial, like hiking, swimming, skiing, and such. Since this biography is going out to your fellow employees, don't use it to sell yourself by telling them how great you are. That will turn off some people. Be informative yet maintain a low-key attitude.

A sample employee profile might include the following:

Your full name
Company name and job title
Colleges you attended and degrees awarded
Prior jobs, if related
Email address and company telephone number
Short biography written in the third person (i.e., use "he" or "she" in describing yourself, never "I," and don't mention anything that can be construed as controversial)

Day One

The big day is here and you are starting your new job. Smile and tell yourself that this will be a great day. Leave home at least an hour before you think you should. Delays happen, and you don't want to be late on your first day. Make it a point to arrive at work fifteen minutes early. Flash a great smile to the doorman, the receptionist, the elevator operator, or anyone else you meet at the company. Introduce yourself and tell them it is your first day. Try to obtain their names. Make a mental note and commit it to paper when possible. Everyone is important, so treat them as such. You never know who can help you (or maybe hurt you) along the way.

When you walk into your work area or office, introduce yourself to the first person you come into contact with. It would not be smart to walk by the office busybody and give her a reason to talk about you. Work environments can be cruel. As you pass by people, tell them who you are and what your job is.

Typically, someone in the office will introduce you to your coworkers. This person now becomes your first friend. Be sure to let him or her know how much their help is appreciated. When you tell people how wonderful they are, it is amazing how smart they think you are. You can't give too much praise during your work life. People want to feel appreciated, and you will continually reap the benefits from making them feel so.

Be a copious note taker. Keep track of names and all you know about those people: Are they married? Do they have children? Remembering their spouse or child's name gives you bonus points. Mentioning a child by name in conversation with a difficult client often broke the ice for me.

Since it is the first day, don't be afraid to ask questions. As mentioned before, some questions are better kept to yourself, especially those that have negative connotations. If the question has the potential to make you appear to be more interested in being away from work than working, don't ask it. You get the idea. When in doubt, don't ask it.

Be a good listener. Look interested even when you're not. Don't give advice about anything. Everyone else in the office knows so much more than you do and it is their chance to shine. Just say thanks for the advice or information given.

Again, remember to thank everyone who helps you. No matter how small the kindness, a thank you is always in order. For the people who are spending a great deal of time with you, a written note of thanks is appropriate.

One good habit to establish starting with your first day at a new job is to not rush out the door at day's end. Whatever time your office typically closes for the day, let's say 5:00 p.m., there will be a mass exodus. Stay around for an additional fifteen minutes or so and someone like your boss will notice. My guess is that the boss doesn't leave at closing time. By staying a little late, it shows you care more about doing your job than getting out of work on time.

To Recap:

- Dress appropriately
- Do some positive visualization (smile and tell yourself that you are going to have a great day)
- Be truthful in all you do and say
- Take a careful look at your benefits package
- Don't use company devices for personal reasons (follow guidelines established by the company)
- Adhere to the company code of conduct
- Prepare your employee online profile carefully
- Leave home an hour earlier than what you think is necessary (arrive at the office fifteen minutes early)
- Introduce yourself to everyone
- Start a notebook with names and details of all the people you meet
- Stay a little late (don't rush out the door at 5:00 with everyone else)

Chapter 2

Now at Work

The orientation is over and it's time to meet with your boss. I'm sure you will quickly learn what the boss expects of all employees. Most companies hire employees with a probationary period, during which time they can discharge you without reason. You can't afford to step out of line during this period.

Job Training

Most likely your boss will assign you a trainer. This person will work very closely with you over the first several days, weeks, or even months on the job. The trainer will regularly report your progress back to the boss. I can't begin to tell you how important this person is to your success. You have great and not-so-great trainers. One of my trainers checked me into a nice hotel on Monday morning and told me to have a great week. I didn't see him again until Friday. This hurt me dearly because I was responsible for learning material at a later date that I should have already known. Needless to say, this person did me no favor. I didn't mention one word of this to the boss. This person was fired within a year for other reasons. Most trainers take their job seriously and use the opportunity as a stepping-stone to management. Whatever the case, let him or her know how much you appreciate the help.

During this initial time on the job, don't move on to something new until you thoroughly understand the task at hand. Never be afraid to ask questions. This might be your only opportunity. If you feel that your progress is slow, acknowledge that and then tell your trainer how much you appreciate his or her patience. Let this person know that you will do whatever it takes to accomplish the task at hand.

Always be upbeat. When the trainer meets with your boss, you want a positive spin on your progress. After a short time, you will have an idea of how well training is going. If everything is great and you are getting positive feedback, give credit to the trainer. A pat on the back goes a long way and is always welcome. If you feel that you are not advancing as quickly as you should, tell the trainer how determined you are to make progress. You must convince the trainer that you are the right person for the job and that you will overcome minor setbacks. It's when times are bad that it is most important to look, feel, and act with confidence. This will get you that second chance.

Believe it or not, training will eventually end, and you will be ready to show the world how capable you are. Make sure, once again, to send each person who helped you a written note of thanks. An email or text message will not suffice. These little gestures make a difference. Then let the boss know how great your trainer was. In doing so, you are telling your boss how smart he or she is for choosing this person.

There are a number of office settings in which personal contact is at a minimum. At some companies all training is done via video conferencing. In this instance it is important to be attentive at all times. You will probably have a written text to follow, and a trainer will point out changes. At the end of the session, this person, or group of people, will usually give you time to ask questions. Take diligent notes and have your questions answered. Again, make note of the trainer's name so you can send a note and offer a thank you for his or her help.

To Recap:

- There is no room for mistakes during probationary period
- The boss will assign you a trainer (this trainer is instrumental to your success)
- This is a great time to ask questions so you clearly understand your responsibilities on the job
- Look for feedback (take appropriate steps whether positive or negative)
- A written note of thanks to your boss, the trainer, and anyone else who helped you at this stage is a must

Chapter 3

Getting Under Way

At this point you will begin your career. Whatever that is, it would be nice to have a trusted friend at your workplace. Try to spend time with your coworkers. Be a great listener, and you'll quickly discover whom you can trust. If someone is badmouthing everyone in the office, he or she will surely do the same to you. Through this process of elimination, you'll find someone you can rely on. This newfound friend can help you with any work problems you might have and keep you on the right track. Thank him or her for their help and ask for suggestions on how you can do your job better.

We all interact with a number of people at work every day. You can't afford to snub anyone, even inadvertently. The doorman you brushed by might know your boss and tell him what a jerk you are. It doesn't take much to be civil to one another. Even though the workday may be chaotic, we must take time to greet everyone with a sincere hello. Being respectful to your coworkers is most important.

Acknowledge the differences you might have with your associates at work. You don't have to agree with someone, but you should honor everyone's opinion. Conflicts in the office usually occur when there is a lack of respect between two people. This happens when business discussions become personal. Avoid this situation at all costs.

After working in the office for a period of time, you will be surprised at the number of shortcuts people have found that will make your job easier. Multiply that by the number of friends you made, and you will be amazed at the amount of information you can collect. This will make you much more efficient at your job.

Establish Good Work Habits

Now might be a good time to talk about work habits. Simple actions will set you apart. For example, always be on time for meetings. I was late for a sales meeting only once in thirty-seven years. It was near the end of my career, and I was only two minutes late. I made sure to always set the hotel room alarm and request a wake-up call from the front desk. Now you can set your cell phone alarm, too. The one time I didn't set the room alarm, the desk forgot to call. You will never know how embarrassed I was. When you go to your next meeting, look around; I guarantee you that a couple of people will walk in late. The boss will also notice. Don't let it be you.

Be at your work area a few minutes early and stay a little later at night. So often a boss needs something done "now." If you are the only person there, the boss will ask you. Over the course of time, you will be doing a number of favors for your boss and maybe your boss's supervisor, just because you are there. Yes, you will be the go-to person. And the fact that you are there when the boss needs you will be remembered. Should there be a layoff, you will not be among the missing due to poor work habits. Who would think that a few minutes here and there could mean so much?

The lack of work ethic in others can give you an advantage. Don't take sick time on Mondays or Fridays, even if you are sick. Go into work and let them see how ill you are and they will send you home. Many people call in sick near the weekend to steal an extra day off. Bosses are not stupid. They know who is trying to extend their weekend and will remember who is habitually doing it. The same goes for breaks and lunch. There are people who extend a fifteen-minute break into a half hour and a half-hour lunch into an hour. Don't do it! This will be another mark against you. Tell your friends and family not to call, email, or text you at work, except in an emergency. This is a big problem in business today. You also don't want to be surfing the Internet for personal reasons. These all have a great effect on overall productivity. The company is paying you for eight hours, not six. Again, it doesn't take people long to figure out who is spending company time talking to friends and doing personal tasks. You may hear that "everyone does it," but that is not true. Regardless, this doesn't make it right.

When business is good, many little items are overlooked. Should sales take a turn for the worse, bosses look for ways to make cuts. If you are someone who the boss can count on to give 100 percent, you will not be the one getting laid off. This is not rocket science! Yet the number of people who just don't understand shocks me.

I remember telling my daughter about going in early and staying late when she was starting a new job. On her third day of work as a speech pathologist, she was putting in an extra fifteen minutes after everyone had left for the day. A big boss she knew from another building came walking through and saw her. The woman asked why she was still there, to which she replied, "Just finishing up some work." The boss mentioned that she was very impressed. I'm sure that incident played some part in her getting the "Staff Recognition Award for Early Intervention" her very first year on the job. She was told that this award is never given to a first-year employee. What happened here is really quite simple. Going above and beyond what is expected will be rewarded.

Another good habit to acquire is complimenting people on a job well done. When the boss singles out a person for doing a good job, be the first to congratulate that person. I don't know of anyone who has ever hurt themselves by praising others. You should be enthusiastic about every success in the office. Enthusiasm is contagious, and you will end up getting your share of praise.

At the end of each day, reflect on what you have accomplished. Think about what you might have done to be more productive. Ask yourself, "Did I handle each situation effectively? Could I have done better?" By doing this daily, you will improve your communication skills and find more positive ways to effectively deal with people.

This is also a good time to look at your schedule for the next day. You should always have a plan for the next workday. Take a few minutes to think about each appointment or job you must complete. If it's an encounter with a person you have previously met, consider how the meeting went and what can be done to make this one more productive. As far as the job you must do, is it something new? If so, think about the materials you need or whom you might need help from. This is a terrific way to end your day. You are leaving work on a positive note and have a great plan for tomorrow.

Now plan a special night for you. It might be having a beer with a friend, a three-mile run in the park, or a great meal with your family. Whatever it is, pat yourself on the back for a job well done. There is no reason you can't pamper yourself in a small way every day. It gives you something to look forward to and you earned it the old-fashioned way, by working hard for it.

To Recap:

- Be a good listener
- Don't overlook anybody (that person might be the one who can help you in the future)
- You can't have enough friends
- Be on time for work and meetings (being there a little early is even better)
- Have a great work ethic (be at work every day and always give 110 percent)
- Praise your fellow workers (they'll remember who their friends are)
- Plan your work and work your plan
- Take some time to pamper yourself

Chapter 4

Move Mountains

How do you move a mountain? One rock at a time! Goals are extremely important to your success in any job. Without them you just move aimlessly along, not accomplishing much. You should have daily, weekly, monthly, and longterm written goals. This will keep you on track. At the same time, this will also force you to put more thought into your projects in order to do a better job. More importantly, this enables you to complete your work on time.

At the start of a new project, examine it carefully. By doing this, you can find out whether the objective is attainable and if the work can be done on time.

Your boss gives you a deadline because he or she has one. When you are late, your boss is late, and not very happy. If you are in the habit of not making deadlines, your tenure will be short-lived. Make your deadlines, exceed your goals, and then submit them to your boss early, as there might be some requested changes.

Companies use team-building concepts to solve a number of problems. This is a great time to show your skills. When an important project comes up, the boss will put together a team to work on it. There is usually a person assigned to dole out responsibilities. Whatever your assignment, it's the success of the project that should be your total focus. This isn't all about you.

After you decide the project is achievable, it's time to work. Now is when your great people skills will be a real asset. Once you begin to work on the assignment, gather input from other team members to make sure you are on the right track. At the same time, offer your help to the other members to build a consensus and bring the project to a successful conclusion. It is extremely important to be able to operate in a team setting because that is what the manager will expect of you. A resumé showing that you were an instrumental part of many successful team projects will give you an edge, should you decide to pursue another job within the company.

Deadlines, Goals, and Approval

Before signing a two-year contract, a purchasing agent asked me how he could be assured that I would do all for his hospital that I was promising. To obtain his signature on this exclusive contract, I agreed to give him written quarterly updates on what I was doing to fulfill my commitment. He signed the contract, and I went above and beyond what I was obliged to do over the next two years. This was done to ensure that the next contract would again go to me. These updates were so successful that other people in my district started doing them. This hospital signed another exclusive contract with me and continued to use my product until I retired.

Talking about team projects makes me think about how important it is to do your job thoroughly. It is not unusual in business for everyone to sign off on a completed project. Occasionally one person will sign off without thoroughly reading it and others will follow blindly. This can bring about a possible disaster. If you are the one to spot the problem after a number of people have signed off on a project, your value to the company will increase considerably. The moral of this story is that you never sign off on anything without thoroughly reading it. You are only doing your job, but there are so many people who do not take the same pride in what they do. Never take shortcuts. If you do, it will come back to bite you.

To Recap:

- Establishing goals is important to your success
- Meeting deadlines improves your job security
- You must be a team player
- Always aim above and beyond what is expected
- Don't ever sign off on anything without thoroughly reading it (I don't care how many people have previously signed off)

Chapter 5

Avoid Office Politics

Office politics is a deadly game with dire consequences. Everyone has opinions on this subject. There are usually a few people who do not like the boss for whatever reason. They will probably tell you all about it. Be a great listener and stay silent. If they ask you directly how you feel about the boss, tell them you are new and haven't had any problems. Then try to change the subject or make up an excuse to leave. They would like nothing better than to drag the new kid into this. The same goes for the self-proclaimed expert on everything. You would think the office couldn't run without this person. Your coworkers will let you know who is carrying their weight and who is not. Again, listen politely and disappear as quickly as possible. People who speak badly of others will more than likely speak ill of you.

Talking about upcoming elections can cost you friends. Your political affiliation is personal. There is no reason to share your views with people in the office. Tell them that you vote for the person you consider the best candidate. A new employee definitely shouldn't push his or her agenda.

I don't know of a person who has too many friends and supporters in the workplace. Your goal should be to make as many as possible. How do you do that? It is quite simple. Convince people that you genuinely care about them. Ask them about their family, dog, cat, or whatever is important to them. Most of us like to talk about family. If all is not going well in a coworker's family, they might be happy to talk to someone about that. This brings up a good point. Should anyone tell you something personal about their family, keep it to yourself. It would be devastating to this person if they found out that you were talking to others about their problems. Others might feel stressed over the amount of work they have. If they do, offer to stay late and help. That's what good friends do, and the favor will likely be repaid should you need assistance in the future.

Not everyone in the office wants to be your friend. Some people just want to do their job and go home. You should respect their wishes.

In any office, the boss has to spend many hours every week dealing with problems between employees. People often stand their ground over issues that could be settled without much fanfare. They dig in, and now the boss has to be involved. Believe me when I tell you that a boss finds this to be a waste of valuable time. You don't want to be a party to this. If you are caught up in an office dispute and there is difference of opinion, take the high road, even if you're right; otherwise, the boss will only remember that the two of you could not solve a simple problem.

Throughout the course of the year, you will be invited to a number of office events. Show up for everything. During my tenure I attended all company events and made a point to talk to everyone. Some people wouldn't go for whatever reason, and the boss would usually take notice. After all, it doesn't look like a team effort if half of your people aren't there. These are the little details that are important to your career. You don't have to stay all night, but at least make an appearance. If someone takes the time to organize an activity for the office, like a ballgame, then try to go. If you can't make it, at least go to the person organizing the event and thank them for taking the time to do so. People deserve to be appreciated. Holiday parties and other events organized by the company are a must to attend. It takes time to organize these events, so volunteer to help. Don't miss a chance to make a good impression. As a new employee, you must always be on your best behavior. People have lost their jobs because of the way they acted at a company party.

To Recap:

- Office politics is a deadly game to be avoided (be a great listener and keep silent)
- Avoid discussing politics
- Always be there for your fellow coworkers
- Steer clear of office conflicts (always take the high road)
- Attend office functions (especially company-planned events)
- Don't embarrass yourself (party later with your friends)

Chapter 6

Step Up to the Plate

There will be a time when the boss needs a favor. Maybe the supervisor of your boss moved an important project up by two months and now your boss is looking for help. This would be a great time to volunteer. Chances are that you will be called on to help anyway. It gives you a great opportunity to demonstrate your skills.

The first action you want to take is to thoroughly examine this undertaking. Ask your boss for suggestions. Try to find out if a project like this has been done before. Check with other departments and some of the veterans for ideas. Organize your thoughts and outline a plan to complete the job on time. Think about any resources you might need from both inside and outside the company.

Getting off to a fast start is essential. Enlist support from your coworkers who have the special skills you need. If it means going to another department or company to receive the help you need, do it now. The sooner you ask for help the better, because you will have time on your side. Now is when you should be putting in the long hours to gain an advantage in organizing your plan of attack.

You need to constantly check on the people helping you. Find out whether they have started and how far along they are. Have a sense of urgency about it. As time goes by, you might have to replace those who are not doing their parts. Don't wait too long. It could jeopardize your deadline.

Even though I am now retired, my friends constantly tell me stories about how people don't meet their deadlines. I find this hard to believe in such a bad job market. I guess lazy people are just that. One friend emailed a coworker and told him that he needed his overdue work in three days or would have to contact his boss. This person didn't acknowledge the email or do the work. After contacting his boss, the work was done. What does that say about this employee? Now you know what not to do. If that boss has to make a decision in the next month about who to lay off in his department, the people not doing the work might lose their jobs.

When the project is completed, take your plan to the boss and someone else you respect and trust. If they both like what you have done, put all the loose ends together in a final report. When complete, sleep on it and then check it over again. If, and only if, you are satisfied, hand in your report and the job is done.

On the other hand, if you have to present your findings at a meeting, you have more work to do. Practice, practice, and then practice more. If you are stumbling along in your presentation, it will not go well, no matter how great the substance. Have all the facts on a slideshow presentation (using software such as PowerPoint) and practice the presentation. Think of all the questions that could be asked, and then make sure you have the answers. Do a dry run in front of a trusted friend and have him or her be very critical, asking all of the questions that may come up during your presentation. When you have ironed out all of the kinks, you are ready.

Once thoroughly prepared, you can proclaim it to be a great day. When presenting, look sharp, smile, and be enthusiastic. Stay on task and respect people's time. Have enough copies of the report for all attending. If you have followed all the steps I just outlined, this will be a very successful meeting. There is no greater satisfaction than a job well done. This will also help to keep your position secure, especially if you are working in a very competitive office.

To Recap:

- Volunteer at the office
- Manage the projects you undertake (get off to a fast start, check on the people helping you, get the job done right, and finish on time)
- Be prepared when making presentations (practice, practice, practice)

Chapter 7

Continue Learning

Look around the office to see what projects need your help. If the job requires a skill that you do not have, talk to your boss about being cross-trained for it. The additional skills you acquire make you more valuable to the organization. There are also many volunteer jobs that have to be done on a weekly or monthly basis. It could be helping the boss with scheduling work, vacation logs, or just about anything else. Learn these jobs so that you can help when needed.

If your company introduces a new procedure, machine, or computer system, one person is usually trained on how to operate the new equipment. In turn, that employee will train the other employees. You want to be this go-to person because it makes your boss's job easier. It will probably mean more work for you, but, again, this makes you more valuable as an employee. This will also give you a chance to network with people from other departments. You might also find out about other openings in the company that haven't been posted yet. Always be positive and enthusiastic so that you make a good impression on everyone you meet. It could be the person you least expect that ends up being a great asset to you.

When my fellow representatives were going on vacation, I would offer to cover their territory should an emergency come up. Their customers would have my number, and one or more of them would always call me for something. This was a great help to a number of different people. When I was going away, these people were lined up to help me. It's funny how this happens.

There is another way in which you can make a valuable contribution to the company. If your workplace needs a notary public or some other position requiring certification, volunteer to obtain that certification during your personal time. Most employers would be willing to pay. This is a big win for both the company and you.

Again, you never have enough education. Take advantage of the funding your company has available for college and graduate courses. They will usually make accessible a certain dollar amount per year and normally require that you obtain a B grade or better to be reimbursed. This is "found money" and you should take hold of it. With the cost of education being so high, why not acquire your education at the company's expense? Should they pay for your college degree or MBA, they will have a vested interest in your success. They may also offer courses directly related to their employees' work in order to increase job performance, and maybe even management courses for a select few. The best way to find out what is available is to talk to your boss or, in a big company, human resources. It makes great sense that all of these degrees and courses will make you more of an asset to your boss and the company. Many people do not take the extra time to improve themselves because it means they must work more hours, nights, or weekends. They are there just to receive a paycheck and stay off the radar screen.

Don't toot your own horn about all you are doing to better yourself. Others in the office might look at your efforts to excel in your job as a threat to theirs. If doing what is right were so easy, everyone would be doing it. Never stop learning. More education could be your key to a brighter future.

To Recap:

- Cross-train to acquire additional skills (this makes you much more valuable to the organization)
- Be the go-to person (when something has to be done, people look to you)
- Take advantage of any educational funding offered by your company (never stop learning)
- Don't toot your own horn (except when meeting with the boss at evaluation time)

Chapter 8

Track Your Progress

Raises are usually tied to goals that you and the boss agree on. Be proactive. When you see that a goal is unrealistic, speak up. The worst idea is to dismiss an unrealistic goal and then worry about it later. This mistake could cost you money. Once you sign off on these goals, you own them. Don't be afraid to adjust a goal.

For example, perhaps you call on sixty customers per month, but your boss wants you to increase that number by 10 percent. You might feel that this is unreasonable, since you make the most contacts in the office. Maybe 5 percent would be more reasonable. Now is the time to speak up and ask for a change. I was never shy at goal-setting sessions because I knew that I would have to live with these decisions that would affect my future raise and bonus.

Something else you can do at this point is to ask the boss if you can revisit these goals should circumstances change. You may find one goal to be unreachable because of situations beyond your control. An example of this is the company losing the bid on a product that was supposed to have sales increases of 10 percent. Also, make sure that your accomplishments, other than goals, will receive careful consideration at evaluation time. If you don't ask, I can assure you that your boss will not offer. It is much easier for the boss to place these goals on your desk and ask you to sign off on them.

You are your own best friend. It is so important to document everything positive in your work life. If you depend on your boss to keep track of all the great deeds you have done in the past three months, six months, or year, you will be seriously short-changed. There should be a file in your desk or on your iPad where you put any piece of information that will help you obtain a raise or promotion. The last item on your agenda every day should be to write down any successes and put it in that file. This is an important habit to develop. Keep track of your other accomplishments. You might have been very instrumental in the success of a big project. Since it technically was someone else's responsibility, maybe the boss doesn't know about your involvement. Write down what you did and how important this was to the project's success.

I remember once finding out early in my career that I was making less than my counterparts who started later. There was a sizable increase in starting salary that put some of these people ahead of me. This was also at a time when I was rated number two in a district of twelve. I always received my raise on the anniversary of my hire. The middle of the year was not the right time to ask for an increase in pay. I did, nonetheless, tell my boss I needed a raise because I was falling behind the new employees and I richly deserved it. He informed me that a raise wasn't possible at this time, but he would talk to his boss. Not only did it happen for the first time I ever remember, but I also received another good raise on my anniversary date. What I want you to take away from this is that rules can be changed when there is good reason for the change. Again, you must be an advocate for yourself.

When you receive an email from someone thanking you for doing something, print it out and put it in your file; otherwise, it will be lost forever. You will not remember six months from now. Think about all of the extras you do in the office. Every time you stay late to help someone with a project, be sure to document it. This is important because it shows you to be a team player. There is probably nothing more important in business today than working as a team for the betterment of the company.

Keep track of the awards and contests that you win. When your reports are on time and you stay within budget, make note of that too. If most of your coworkers take sick time and you don't, make mention of the fact that you are there every day and on time. The boss might think this to be important, and it could make a difference when it comes time to getting a raise. Don't overlook the extra work you did at night and on weekends to help the boss make his deadlines.

Last, but not least, please do not forget about those goals. That is the first item the boss will look at when you have your evaluation. Check on your goals weekly and monthly to make sure you are on track. Don't wait until the last minute to have a goal changed because it will be too late. When you are two months into your goals, it is a great time to assess whether they are all realistic. If you find one that is not, talk to the boss about changing it, and have a good substitute goal for the boss' consideration.

Make it easy for the boss to help you. Exceed your goals. After all, the boss wants you to succeed.

To Recap:

- Carefully select your goals
- Adjust or change goals depending on circumstances (don't wait until the end of the year)
- Constantly check on your progress
- Exceed your goals

Chapter 9

Know Your Boss

The more you know about the people you work for, the easier it is to please them. You must gain every advantage possible to be truly successful. Gathering information is not very difficult to do. First of all, the company might have an informational website for its employees. This could tell you about your boss's education, hobbies, and more.

Be careful about the information people don't give you. I can remember calling on a nurse and new mother, whom I will call Karen Duggan. One month later I met another nurse who was about the same age in another town. Let's say her name is Pat Duggan. Talking with her I asked if she was related to Karen Duggan, thinking they might be sisters. She said, "Karen is my wife." To that I replied: "She is a great nurse," and congratulated her on their new baby. Never assume anything.

I had one boss who wanted to see a very clean and well-organized car when he worked with you. All of your samples were to be neatly placed in the trunk of your car along with well-organized informational brochures for all of our products. If you did this, he was sure to have a great day. These are the easy parts of the job that you should not overlook. Selling all day is hard. Keeping your car neat is not.

Look for activities that you have in common with your superiors, like hiking or biking. Make a note of a partner's name. Know the names of the children, dogs, cats, or birds.

How to Learn More

The secretary or administrative assistant can be a wealth of information. Who knows the boss better than this person? The assistant has more influence than most people know. When personnel decisions are being made, there is a good chance the boss will ask the assistant for input. This person can also let you know if there is a problem brewing, long before it surfaces publicly. What you don't want to do is start asking too many questions about the boss.

You can also tell much about a person by looking at his or her desk. If the desk is always neat and organized, that tells you that you might want to tidy up your own desk. Some bosses only care about results. If so, focus on your goals and make sure that you exceed most of them.

How old is your boss? The older ones are less likely to rock the boat, especially if close to retirement. Consider whether upper management is open to constructive criticism. Some companies look at it as negativity. If they do, don't offer it.

Once again you should also look at the dress of your coworkers. If it is on the conservative side, follow their lead. Some bosses want you in the office every day and on time. If that is important to your boss, do it. When upper management wants green fire engines, that's what you give them.

Don't ever assume that you know something and then act on it. I can remember once asking a gentleman, who was new to my area, what his name was. He told me that his name was Kevin O'Connor, to which I replied, "It is great to meet a good Irishman like myself." Surprisingly, he told me that he was not Irish but Jewish and from New Jersey. I never did ask him how he ended up with a name like that, but I did learn a very valuable lesson. I hope that by now you realize how important it is to obtain as much accurate information as you can about everyone you work with. The more you know, the easier it is to deal with them.

Exercise

Write out what you know about the people at work. Now name five additional things you would like to know about each person. Would this additional information make your relationship with each person better? I think so.

To Recap:

- Gather information on your boss (education, family, hobbies, etc.)
- Never assume anything (know the facts)
- Follow the boss's lead (If he wants green fire engines, give him green fire engines)
- Never be critical of your boss
- Information is power

Chapter 10

Understand Pricing Agreements & Contracts

For those of you who may deal with pricing agreements and contracts, we are living in a new age. There is a big difference between the two. Pricing agreements usually guarantee you something at a given price for a period of time. It is not usually an exclusive arrangement, and both parties might have an out with thirty or sixty days of notice. You don't have to put as much time into making a decision about most pricing agreements, especially if you have an out. However, most contracts today can be ironclad, if you want them to be. What you expect in a contract must be clearly defined, or the likelihood of you getting it is slim.

You must completely read and understand the contracts you sign. Should the contract to purchase your office printer be forty pages long and full of ambiguity, don't sign it. Tell the salesperson exactly what you don't like about it, and you will be amazed at how quickly the language in the contract changes. For example, "limited warranty" means just that. They will probably give you a discount on parts and labor, which really means not much of a guarantee at all.

Some contracts are downright outrageous. They might put in a clause that states you must notify the company sixty days in advance of contract expiration as to whether you will continue with them. If you don't notice that in the contract and sign it, you might be under contract for an additional two years at a 10 percent increase.

In this age of intense competition, the written word is more powerful than the spoken one. Should you be the person in the office in charge of all the equipment contracts, this is your chance to shine. Don't let people rush you into signing anything. This will only lead to trouble. You should communicate which parts of the contract are not acceptable and ask to have those removed. If the representative won't do it, someone else will. Be sure to obtain a few different quotes. Examine them carefully and consider both quality and price. If it's a new company, beware of all the promises and consider whether or not those promises are realistic. You don't want to buy a new computer system from a company that might be out of business next month. My best advice is to move slowly and bring a number of people into the process. These decisions affect everyone in the office.

On the other hand, if you are the one offering the pricing agreement or looking to have a contract signed, be sure to deal with the decision-maker. Pricing agreements can usually be handled quickly. Contract negotiations can take a great deal of time, and you must be talking to the person who will be signing on the dotted line. With that said, it's a good idea to aim high.

For example, if my client wanted a two-year contract, I would also offer a longer-term contract as an alternative that would protect their price or give them some other advantage. Of course, when it came time to sit down with the decision-maker, I would try to get his or her signature for the longer period (e.g., four years instead of two). They can only say yes or no. In my experience, when a company signed for the longer period, it made me a hero and my boss very happy. Whenever they signed for the lesser commitment, it was still a big win.

Work with the Decision-Maker

So often people are talking to the person they think is making the decision. If this person is not the one signing the contract, find the person who is. You must have all your supporters firmly in your camp before you go in and ask for a signature. If you can't obtain an autograph right away, find out why and then tie it up quickly. The longer a contract or agreement goes unsigned, the less likely it will ever happen. When the agreement or contract is finally signed, don't consider it done. Many signed contracts are undone during implementation.

To avoid losing a contract during implementation, immediately let the people who are affected know that the contract is signed. Tell them that you will be there every step of the way to help them make the necessary changes. Then you must follow through and be there to answer all of their questions. Great follow-up prevents problems that could derail the contract. Usually a couple of weeks after implementation, the dust will settle and then you can pat yourself on the back.

Know the End User

Contracts and agreements that you enter into are very important to your company. When there is a great deal of money at stake, all involved must come to a consensus before making a decision.

For example, you may be placed on a committee in charge of coming up with a computer system that will do more and save time. Should it do everything you thought it would and increase productivity by 10 percent, all is well. If it doesn't work out, the committee will take the fall.

Typically, implementing a new computer system requires the input of an IT person or employee with considerable computer experience. This person will often head such projects. The IT person will look at a number of different systems, and then receive input from the people who will be most affected.

I can't tell you how often a computer system has been changed in an organization or office without the users being consulted or at least asked for their opinion. When this happens, chaos is sure to occur. Usually, programming changes must be made to adapt the system to what the people need. This results in a loss of precious time. If everyone on the committee does their job right the first time, this project will be successful.

To Recap:

- Pricing agreements are usually very flexible
- Pricing contracts are usually ironclad
- "Limited warranty" means just that (maybe a discount on parts and labor but not much more)
- Don't sign any contract that is ambiguous (make the company redo it to your liking)
- When offering a contract, deal with the decision-maker (that would be the person who is designated to sign the contract)
- Come to a consensus with the people affected before buying or leasing a piece of equipment for the office

Chapter 11

Be Efficient

Being efficient is all about the proper use of time. There is no reason you can't do 25 percent more work than your coworker if you use your time effectively.

Handle Jobs Once

While in the office, handle jobs once. If you are reading an email, looking at a text message, or taking a call about something that someone wants, do it now. That way you won't have to make a note of it and read it six times before doing it. Procrastination can make a job overwhelming.

Make a Schedule—Then Stick to It!

Increasing productivity is instrumental to your success and that of the company. Scheduling your work is essential. You are most productive when you have a time schedule.

Make sure you are prepared for all meetings. Have an agenda and make sure that the person you are meeting knows what the agenda is. When both are prepared, there is a better chance that you will achieve the desired results. After a day of meetings, you should sit down and look at what was accomplished. Try to schedule a time to tie up the loose ends, while the information is fresh in your mind.

In my case, I would be driving all day. On my way home at night, I would always pull over to park somewhere. The reason for this was to finish up any paperwork I had to do and then make any last-minute calls. I would then sit there with my computer and plan the next day. Once that was done, I would go home. What takes me thirty minutes to do on the road would tie me up for two hours at home. Also, I could give my wife and kids the undivided attention they deserve.

Upon arrival at your office the next morning, immediately take care of any problems that occurred during the night. This will make your day so much easier. Now you can pay close attention to your schedule.

Make Your Meeting Meaningful

Unless you are expecting an important call, turn your cell phone off during meetings. You can then pay careful attention to the matters at hand. Also, it's a common courtesy to give full attention to the people you are meeting with.

When discussing issues in a meeting, you must be decisive. If a decision is called for, don't ever say, "I don't care" or "it doesn't matter to me." If you do, you are saying that the time we spent together is worthless. Meetings should be about expectations, and you should be prepared to solve a problem or put together a plan to accomplish something.

In the office setting you'll notice that many impromptu meetings pop up only to end in a waste of your time. If someone calls to set up a meeting now, it's generally our tendency to meet with the person because we assume the issue at hand is important. When someone calls and asks to meet "now," this might be a good time to inquire what they need to see you about. Even the boss might be happy to reschedule, if you are busy. On the other hand, maybe the meeting is crucial and timely.

The bottom line is: no one knows the boss better than you do; and it's important not to let people disrupt your day over trivial matters. You can't let people steal precious time, because you never get it back. Just five minutes of stolen time per day translates to nearly three days per year. Multiply that by the number of people in the office and that is a real loss in productivity.

When you're efficient, you accomplish more than your

coworkers. This makes you a very valuable employee. It is most important to develop these habits early in your career so that they become second nature. Should there be people reporting to you some day, they will imitate what you do and not what you say.

To Recap:

- Procrastination can make a job overwhelming (do it now)
- Schedule your work day
- Be prepared for all meetings
- Meetings should be about expectations (be prepared to make a decision)
- Don't let people steal your time (stay the course)

Chapter 12
Develop Your Network

There is too much going on in this ever-changing business environment to do your job well without help. The resources you need might be within your own department. When you are working on a project and seem to be hitting a dead end, talk to coworkers. They might have the expertise you need. If not, chances are the company has other departments that might be dealing with similar projects. Ask around.

Your next step is to check with other businesses in the area that do similar work. Drop by a non competitive company and introduce yourself. Make new friends and maybe solve your problem. The worst-case scenario is that you have a couple of new contacts.

I definitely used networking to my advantage. In sales you come across people every day who have problems in their office or institution. In one case a doctor group needed coverage for their patients at a hospital in a nearby state. They did not have hospital privileges there and needed a local pediatric practice to see their patients. After one of the doctors informed me about the situation, I informed him that I would take care of his problem. This was not part of my job. But by networking with a sales representative in that state, I was able to find a coverage group to see their patients. This was a tremendous help and made me much more valuable to that office than my competitor. Networking to help my clients is one of the reasons for my success.

Networking Via the World Wide Web

The Internet is our greatest source for networking today. Go online and look up a networking group in your field, preferably one nearby that meets on a regular basis. Search for business networking, and you will see a number of group websites where you can enroll as a member. List your name, business, and location, and you will be linked with the particular group. If no group fits your business needs, form your own. Note that group affiliations on websites are open to anyone; so don't give out sensitive information.

If you do find the information to solve your work problem on the Internet, be sure to tell the boss. This shows how resourceful you are and your boss will remember that at raise time. You always receive extra credit when you think outside of the box.

Benefits of Networking

Networking is not only a good way to solve problems, but it's also great way to find a new job. Let's say your spouse is getting transferred to Florida and you need to find a new job. Check with your company first about possible openings in that area. If none are available, join a networking group in Florida and see if there are any opportunities in your field.

Maybe you like hiking but have no one to go with. By networking, you can find a group near you that does the kind of hiking you like. This is one more way that the Internet can be of service to you. With all the demands on our time, we all find it important to look for new ways of doing things. Once you go onto a networking site that you find helpful, share it with friends. Whether they are interested or not, they will appreciate your caring. Networking is instrumental to your success in the workplace.

The Internet isn't the only place to network. You could meet with a group of friends and start a stock club. Everyone invests five hundred dollars, and the group takes a vote on when to buy and sell stock. Each person is responsible for doing research on stocks to buy and then presents the findings to the group. This is a fun way to learn about investing and you might even make some money.

To Recap:

- Network to your advantage (in this ever-changing business environment, we all need help)
- Use the Internet (greatest source of knowledge available)
- Coworkers (including those working in other departments), people at other companies, and friends are all valuable assets
- Networking solves others' problems and has career and personal benefits for you

Chapter 13

Balance Job & Life

The workplace of today is so different from that of ten years ago. We are in a global market and technology is changing everything at lightning speed. You must be willing to do more on the job. What this means is that you, not the company, will be responsible for your future success. This said, it's important to work at a job you like. If not, make a change to something better suited to you. It's imperative to make such a move before you invest too much time.

Figure out just how much effort you are willing to put into your work. If you want to do an adequate job, you can usually do that without committing extra hours to the company. In this business environment you must be at work every day, be prompt, don't make waves, and help out when times are tough. Most good employees fall into this category and will do well. However, in tough times, this might not even be enough to prevent you from being laid off.

Reduce Stress

To keep your job and life in balance, find a way to reduce stress at work. This might mean leaving the building at lunchtime just to escape for a half hour or so, or taking a ten-minute break to listen to music (something soothing or rock—whatever you fancy). With the iPod and so many other devices on the market, it's easy to have your favorite tunes readily available.

When the workplace is too stressful, find a reason to leave. Volunteer for projects outside the workplace. There are times when you need some separation from the office.

This change will be a great mental health break.

Plan your days off just after high-stress times; usually the last day of the month or the end of the quarter. Then you will take a break when you most need it.

Work On Good Communication

If you are overly anxious for whatever reason, it's important to remember that the boss needs good people like you. Talk to your boss about your concerns and attempt to work things out. Be enthusiastic and upbeat at all times.

Now, if your goal is to climb the corporate ladder, it will take much more than just extra time. You must be willing to make a major commitment. If single, you are the only person that must be consulted. However, if you are married or have a partner, then you must sit down and see if both are on the same page. You must be perfectly honest about the time commitment that must be made and reach an agreement before deciding your career path. Also, factor in the time spent away from the family. A number of developmental positions require travel. If children are involved, both parties must be willing to make the necessary sacrifices for you to succeed.

My wife and I had this conversation about me climbing the corporate ladder. I had three little girls at the time and did not want to miss their growing up. Most promotions at that time meant many overnights away from the family. I liked my present job and didn't want to travel. This enabled me to be home and spend more time with my family. This also gave me a chance to coach all three of my girls' sports teams, which I did. I always felt that I made the right decision to remain a sales representative.

If you decide to move up in the organization, it can be done successfully. However, it does take a measure of work. You need great organizational skills (or you better develop them quickly). In addition, working long hours requires you to take care of yourself. Eat right, exercise, and make time for your family. When you are away from home on a work assignment for five days or more, I wouldn't advise you to play golf on the weekend.

Whatever you do, stay healthy and make time for yourself and the family. Your spouse and children deserve some quality time. Don't waste it arguing over petty issues. You must spend time with your children. They need your love and attention. Let the people who are closest to you know how important they are. Doing this on a consistent basis is a wonderful gift and will be very helpful in making you successful both at work and home.

When not working, you and your partner should be there for each other, both mentally and physically. It is better to stay late at the office and finish your work than to come home and sit down at your desk. Your time at home should be family time. Remember to ask your partner about his or her day, and then listen. You should ask, "How can I help you?" It might be fixing dinner or giving the kids a bath. By addressing these needs, you are going to make your life easier in the long run.

All of this is not only good for your relationship, but it's also important for your well-being. All work and no personal life will wear you out. When you or your partner are at wits end, it's time to clear the schedule and take a few days off. Make sure this time is devoted to family.

If all is not well on the domestic front, talk to your boss and be very candid. Tell him that you must travel less and spend more time at home. This might slow you down, but most bosses will understand. It is better to have a happy employee working regular hours than to have a distraught one working many more. Being honest with everyone is another great way to keep your job.

To Recap:

- The workplace of today is radically different
- Logging in extra hours are a must
- Keep your job and life in balance by first reducing stress and improving communication
- Climbing the corporate ladder requires a major commitment
- Stay healthy and make time for yourself
- Family time should be just that

Chapter 14

Lead by Example

What you do is much more important than what you say. We have all heard the expression that he or she talks a great game. No one wants to be that person. If you are, no one will be listening or taking you seriously when you have something important to say.

There is great evidence from the beginning of time that when you lead by example, people follow. The great military commanders led their men to victory against incredible odds, only because the men believed in them.

Put Your Words into Action

When working in an office, you send out signals by what you do more than by what you say or think. The way you dress might signal your work ethic, whether that be right or wrong. By dressing neatly, with well-groomed hair and polished shoes, most people will think of you as organized. This might not be true, but human nature takes over and people make judgments based on what they see.

Take pride in yourself. Think before you act. You want to be the person in the office that all new employees look up to. Doing your job the right way isn't easy but can be very rewarding. Even though you are not the boss, you are surely a leader, in every sense of the word, when you do your job right. This also makes you a very valuable employee.

Carefully consider every move. If you want to be the boss, a successful team leader, or a valued employee, develop the relevant good habits early. It is vital that you set a good example from the very start. An individual who takes all the allotted sick time, comes to work late, takes long breaks and lunch hours, and then by luck becomes team leader, has a problem. This person's colleagues know that he or she doesn't deserve the promotion. Don't ever expect the coworkers to make a person in that situation look good. Such a person has not earned the respect.

Let's say you are the one who has done everything right, and then you become a team leader or the boss. Most coworkers will follow your lead. The reason they will is that you have earned their respect through example.

I can remember people asking me about a hard-nosed boss that I knew very well. My answer was always the same. "She expects her people to work hard and put in extra hours when necessary. If you do what she asks, she will be your biggest supporter. She plays no favorites." What more can you expect from a boss?

Be Positive

As an employee in charge of a project, always be constructive. When discussing the job at hand, emphasize how important it is to the future of the company. Always be upbeat and stress to your coworkers that you are confident that your group can complete the job successfully and on time. Let them know that you are all in this together. If plans don't move along quickly and the project is running behind, you can always lower the bar.

A department that runs on mutual respect gets the best results. Be forgiving. People make mistakes, and when they do, it gives you a chance to gain their trust. One must be a good listener. Once you discuss a problem, make sure all agree on the remedy. Then, let it go.

Maybe, in the heat of the moment, one of your coworkers makes some nasty comments that truly hurt you. Sit down and talk about it. Maybe this person has family problems and uncontrollably lost it momentarily. Some bosses can't forgive and forget, but no one wants to be constantly reminded of a stupid mistake. If handled properly, this person could become one of your best employees.

A leader has no time for grudges. In the heat of the moment, we have all made statements that we regret. That goes for bosses, too. When this happens, they should acknowledge it. Maybe the boss said exactly what was called for. If that is the case, let it be. However, if the boss thinks something you said is uncalled for, apologize and admit that you are wrong.

Being the boss means that your main concern should be the good of the company. Getting the job done is most important. Lead by example and others will follow.

To Recap:

- What you do is more important than what you say
- Take pride in everything you do
- Carefully consider every move you make
- Be positive and constructive
- Be a good listener
- Lead by example and others will follow

Chapter 15

Solve Problems

Worrying doesn't solve problems and can be hurtful to your well-being. The stress worry creates is not only bad for your heart, but it's thought to be a contributing factor in many forms of cancer and other diseases. We worry because we have a problem that we don't have an answer to. So our first inclination is to think about all of the negative consequences that could result from this. It's amazing how many terrible events can happen to you as a result of one problem if you worry long enough about it.

Take, for example, getting a call from an important client or boss. They leave you a message to call them. An optimist might think that something good has happened and the boss wants to share the good news. Or maybe the client is calling with an order for some additional business. On the other hand, a call like this puts the worrier in a panic. The worrier thinks of everything that could have gone wrong and then, even without foundation, might even think his or her job is in jeopardy. Negativity sets in.

Stay Optimistic & Be Proactive

I was usually very optimistic but had one such client who made me very uneasy. Every time he called, it was a problem. This happened to be an account that I did a great deal of business with. It was getting near contract renewal time when I heard his voice on my answering machine. "Please call me." Panic set in and I didn't call him back for hours. I thought it had to be that they were not going to renew my contract. Finally, I decided to call him. What he wanted was some free samples for a friend. Instead of calling him back right away, I let this call paralyze me for four hours.

Without even knowing why the client called, the worrier thinks about how to make up for imaginary losses. It's important to take action when a situation like this occurs. Return the call immediately and expect the best. Whatever you do, don't start off the conversation with, "What is the problem?" If you do, the person on the other end might come up with one.

When a problem arises at work, address it as such and clearly define it; then sit down and think about how to solve it. Often there is a readymade solution that is not too painful. Make the decision and move on to other matters.

One major worry in the workplace today is sickness. Most employers have very limited sick days, if any. If you are married and have children, this is a big problem. For this reason there are too many people going to work when they should be staying home. My advice to anyone suffering from an ailment that impairs the ability to work is to immediately talk to your boss. Let him know that you have this problem and are getting treatment. Also assure him that you will stay late and work weekends or do whatever it takes to make sure your work is done. Be proactive. Don't let the boss find out that you are taking excessive breaks and not getting your job done—then it might be too late.

Create a Realistic Solution & Timetable

Don't try to solve a problem by putting a Band-Aid on it. The problem will only come up again and take more of your time. Instead, come up with a realistic solution and then create a timetable to achieve it.

Some problems are very real and complex. If that is the case, a timetable is crucial. If the crisis is crippling your operation, worrying about it won't help. Bring in your best people or consultants from the outside, those with expertise in this area. You must inject a sense of urgency into the situation so that work on solving the problem starts immediately.

Should you be leading the team, make sure all possible solutions are explored. For example, if a major piece of equipment goes down, you have to consider the cost and time it will take to fix it (or whether it can be fixed at all). Another group can look into buying or leasing new equipment. Someone else can look into the cost of outsourcing the work. There should be a deadline for the proposed solution and a cost estimate. Then a decision must be made. This sure beats worrying about it.

Worrying is inaction that takes on a life of its own and can undermine both you and your company. There is only so much time you can spend on a problem. It might be that you can't afford the solution. This is important to know when the time comes. There is a great deal of energy that goes into solving problems. When that energy can be better used somewhere else, it is time to move on.

True problem-solvers are great assets to any company.

To Recap:

- Worrying solves nothing
- When confronted with a problem, take action now (don't let panic set in)
- Be proactive (don't let circumstances dictate outcomes)
- Project leaders must be able to make decisions
- Problem-solvers are a great asset to any company

Chapter 16
Be Resourceful

While working at your present job, you may run into problems where you need to consult outside resources. Probably the greatest resource available is the Internet. The World Wide Web can be a problem-solver's best friend. There is no subject in the world that the Internet doesn't have adequate information on. The biggest problem with the Internet is that anyone can set up a website to distribute "expert" information—even if this person is not an expert. Therefore, you can receive some bogus information. Check your sources carefully. Also, have the information confirmed by someone else, if possible. In the case of a company background check, you can contact the Better Business Bureau.

Depending on what you are looking for, the library is also a great resource. Most libraries have a resource librarian who will be only too happy to help you. The best time to contact librarians is early in the morning, before they become involved in other projects. I can't begin to tell you how much time a good librarian can save you.

When searching for current (or recent) information, you should go to a major bookstore and browse through periodicals, magazines, and books in the business section. You should also talk to a knowledgeable clerk who can check to see what resources are available on a particular subject. They can then place a special order for you, if necessary.

The Internet book sites, such as Amazon.com, have thousands of titles available. It's often hard to determine whether a book is helpful until you buy it. Make sure Internet sites you order from are secure before you give credit card information.

Feel free to visit your local college or business school

library, if you are fortunate enough to have access to one. They have textbooks on most business subjects, business magazines, and journals. Their resource people are usually very capable.

Should the problem be complex and there are many aspects to deal with, you might have to put together a team to handle it. Whatever resource(s) you decide to use, always keep your goal in sight. It is not about you and the glory (so don't go around bragging about all the extra work you're doing to research the topic at hand). Getting the job done is essential. That is what the boss expects from you.

Job Change Resources

To deal with personal issues, there are also many resources available. If you find that your job is not working out, it might be time to make a change. If you are happy with the company, but not your situation, you might want to seek out other opportunities within your organization. Match your skills with jobs available and set up an appointment with someone in human resources. The HR staff will look at your personal file. This will go a long way in determining whether you have a shot at the desired job. Being a model employee is a tremendous help during this time.

Never mention to anyone at work that you are dissatisfied with your job; and don't tell people you are looking for another one. Your best friend at work will likely only tell their best friend and so on. Everyone will know within a week. Your job could end up being in jeopardy. Instead of coworkers, think of your friends who work elsewhere. They might have openings where they work and could give you important information about their business.

Another resource that people overlook is college alumni

(or the alumni office). They might be able to match you up with successful graduates who live in your city. Personnel in the alumni office are usually only too willing to help.

Remember, it's so much easier to find a job when you already have one. Continue to work very hard at your present position because it might take time to find your next one.

I never proclaimed myself to be the smartest person in the company, but no one could outwork me. When a problem came up, I always knew where to look for help or who to ask. There was always a sense of urgency, and I thought about the consequences should I not be able to solve it. If the problem was a contract breaker, everything else was put aside until the problem was resolved. On the other hand, if the problem was not of real consequence, I didn't spend as much time on it. You must learn how to prioritize your time to take advantage of the best available resources.

To Recap:

- Consult outside resources when needed (Internet, libraries, book stores, etc.)
- Check validity of information received
- A resource librarian can save you a great deal of time
- Visiting the business section of a bookstore could be helpful
- The HR department is the best resource for personnel issues
- Friends outside of the office are good resources when looking for a new job (don't consult with coworkers)
- Collect necessary information to make a decision and then move on

Chapter 17
Think Positive

Positive thinking has been addressed throughout this book in various contexts, but it is such an important topic that an entire chapter is devoted to it here. Our minds control who we are and what we do. That is why it's so important to program your mind for success. We often hear how it's essential to have goals, because without them we will move aimlessly through life. While this is true, writing down a number of goals and taping them to your mirror is not a job well done. Some people think that by looking at their goals every day, they will eventually accomplish them. That is not the case. What you need is a well thought-out plan on how and when to reach each one of your goals. A plan without a date might end up being a lifetime goal. What we do every day in our mind should help us accomplish our goals in a timely manner. Remember, your plan is just a blueprint, and it can be changed at any time.

Another key aspect is to be persistent. I remember once finding out that a doctor client of mine, whom I had called on for some twenty years, had recently changed his orders at the local hospital to my competitor's product. At first I could not believe that he would do this after all my years of excellent service. He was not only a client, but I had considered him a good friend. When I confronted him at his office and asked why he did this, he answered that there was no choice. One of my competitors came into his office and told my physician that her job might be in jeopardy if she didn't pick up some business.

First of all, I assured the doctor that no representative was going to lose their job because one doctor didn't change his orders. I also reminded him of all that I did for his patients over the years. The doctor felt badly that he made the change, but didn't want to look foolish to the hospital by changing his orders once again. He promised me that in six months he would change his orders back to my product. I expressed that this would not be fair to me because I earned and deserved his support now. Exasperated, the doctor left the room. I was determined to stay there until he changed his orders back to my product. Fifteen minutes later he came back to his office to see me still sitting there.

At this point he asked, "You aren't going to leave until I change my orders, are you?"

I said, "No, I'm not."

With that, he took out his pen and wrote a new order for my product and never changed it again. This happened because I had a long-term relationship of great service and he knew I deserved his business. However, as you can see, it doesn't happen unless you persist. That was a very gratifying moment for me.

The moral of this story is to think positive and be persistent. Never give up. This will help you achieve great success. If there is a business slowdown, your job will be secure.

You must persevere in order to be successful. Negativity starts to set in when a job becomes difficult. Our mind begins to tell us all the reasons why our plan will not work. This is when you have to stop and reprogram it. Think of all the reasons why it will work. This is not an easy switch to make, but positive thoughts are vital to your success. What will help you is one of the hundreds of books or CDs on positive mental attitude. Just a few minutes of reading or listening to advice on positive thinking daily will make a difference. Your brain needs positive feedback to help carry you on to victory. We all need some help. It has often been said that if you make the people around you successful, you will become successful yourself. I believe that to be true, and so it all starts with you.

Focus on your strengths. You might have great communication skills. If so, volunteer to do the group presentations and lead discussions, when appropriate. Everyone has strengths, but strengths are only an asset if used to your advantage.

Fear is an obstacle, and it can be very destructive. Whether others think your fear is irrational doesn't matter. It is real to you. Don't let fear paralyze you. You must face your fears and take steps to deal with them.

Exercise:

Take a moment to write down your fears. Now, write down how each fear affects you. After looking over your list, think long and hard about how you might triumph over these fears. Sometimes the process of putting them down on paper and reading them makes your fears less scary. Then share these concerns with the people you love and respect. Ask them for their support in overcoming these fears so you can move on to achieving your goals. This could take time, and you may even need professional help. The important part is to conquer your fears and move on.

Finally, failure is a fact of life and you will experience it along the way. If you are afraid to fail, you won't make the tough decisions that set you apart. Most inventors experience failure many times before they succeed. Failure just brings you one step closer to your next success.

There are no shortcuts to success. You can't succeed in your job without maintaining a positive mental attitude. It also contributes to a much happier personal life.

To Recap:

- Program your mind for success
- Plan your work and then follow the plan
- Persistence pays off—never give up
- Think positive (reflect on all the reasons why something should work)
- Remember: failure brings you one step closer to your next success

Chapter 18

Support Your Coworkers

You come into and go out of this life alone. For the rest of it, you will need support. A good means of getting this is to be an enthusiastic supporter of your coworkers. Always look for ways to help. This action, on your part, will not go unnoticed by the people you work with. These same people will be there at a moment's notice, should you need some assistance.

Smile and be enthusiastic in all that you do. Nobody wants to work with the office complainer. Just take one day in your life and live it with a continuous smile on your face and enthusiasm in your voice. Witness the results.

When I go into my local coffee shop, there is always a line and people are often in a hurry. Most customers don't address the workers by name, even though they all wear nametags. When it is my turn to order, I always address the workers by name and usually tease them about something. I'll ask, "What does one have to do to get some service around here?" I do this with a big smile and it usually changes the whole mood of the place. The people in line are now all laughing. The workers enjoy the light moment, and I love doing it.

Start at the coffee shop with a big smile and exuberant "hello!" when you walk through the door; and then continue on through the day like that. I can guarantee that if you do this for a few days, it will become a habit. The response you receive from people will convince you of that.

Give and Thou Shall Receive

We all want to be loved and treated with respect. To receive love and respect, you must give it. This is not only important on the job, but throughout life. Most people are too busy in their own lives to consider the feelings of others (much less everyone they meet). Everyone you come into contact with will welcome your positive attitude.

There is much that happens in an office during the course of the week. You should make it a point to applaud people when they do something right. At the same time, if someone in the office makes a big mistake, do your best to support him or her. At some point you will be that person making a mistake. Most importantly, do not be part of the group that is critical. Ganging up on someone in this situation is taking the low road and could be devastating to that person.

I can remember when a great friend of mine, and a fellow sales representative, was moving quickly up the ladder in my company. You couldn't help but be an enthusiastic supporter of this guy. He was bright, friendly, and ambitious. We would get together whenever possible, which was usually at big meetings. I still recall telling him once to "keep moving because it is difficult to hit a moving target." Move is what he did. He ended up becoming the president of my division. He never did forget that I was his friend from the very beginning.

Business is changing quickly because of the immediate access of information through the Internet. Long-term planning is, in some cases, a three-month window. What hasn't changed is the need for people to feel appreciated. Take time out of your busy day to care about the people you work with. When you enter meetings, go out of your way to make each person feel special. Instead of talking business, you may extend a personal compliment (e.g., on someone's nice earrings) or congratulations (e.g., on a new home or baby). This has nothing to do with work or productivity, yet makes people feel good, and that is important.

It is easy to find flaws in anyone's character if that is

what you are looking for. Instead, you should be searching for the good in everyone you work with. This will pay dividends for a long time.

There are a number of people who get lost in the shuffle. These are the quiet ones who just do their job well every day. Because they do what is expected of them, the boss might not give them special recognition. Everyone needs to know that what they do makes a difference. Take matters into your own hands and give those employees a pat on the back. If they don't receive positive feedback from the people they work with, it's hard to continue. When you are enthusiastic about something, it becomes contagious. If someone is promoted, bring in balloons and a card. Have everyone in the office sign it. Tell the person how excited everyone is for them. This way it becomes a joyous moment for the whole office.

On another note, people don't want to hear about how wonderful you are. That is not how you obtain respect from the people you work with. You get it the old-fashioned way, by working hard. If you are doing a great job, they already know. The only time you should be selling yourself is at evaluation time, when you sit down with your boss.

As a part of the team, try to accentuate the positive and not dwell on the negative. When someone has an idea that you support, let him or her know it. When there is something brought up that you know won't work, be more careful. Take the person aside and offer other suggestions. Don't ever embarrass an employee in front of a group. I have seen this happen all too many times. People make statements that they later regret. That is not a good way to make friends.

One other person you can't forget is the boss. He or she is responsible for all that happens. When your boss comes up with a plan that you think is workable, let him or her know it. Bosses are not unlike you and me, and they, too, need to receive support and appreciation from other people. At the same time, should you think the boss's plan is unworkable, don't communicate all the reasons why something won't work. A boss doesn't need more problems. The best alternative is to take the plan and note the perceived necessary changes to complete the assignment. When you go to the boss with a problem and a solution, he or she is more likely to listen. After all, your boss just wants the job done. Remember, passionate supporters are vital to the success of any company.

To Recap:

- Everyone needs support
- Smile and be enthusiastic (both are contagious)
- Consider the feelings of others
- Applaud the success of coworkers
- People need to feel appreciated
- You earn respect by working hard
- Support the ideas of your coworkers
- Don't ever embarrass an employee in front of others
- Passionate supporters are vital to the success of any company

Chapter 19

Create Your Good Luck

We hear this all the time. He or she is so lucky. The boss loves him. She can do no wrong. I'm sure you have a number of other ways to describe how some of your friends got the big raise or promotion. Even if you keep it to yourself, you might think that they are lucky. Luck is a possibility, but more than likely someone received that raise or promotion because they earned it. When an opportunity comes your way and you do everything in your power to prepare yourself for it, you might get lucky too.

Most of the lucky people I know worked very hard to be successful. Look at the lucky person who is a doctor. They had to attend and graduate from college, four years of medical school, and three to five years of residency (or more) before they were done. Then they had to pass board exams. So, after all these years they are now somehow lucky? The same goes for the lucky lawyers and the lucky CEOs. Most of these people sacrificed a long time in order to be "lucky."

Voice Your Goals & Work Hard

If you are looking for a promotion or different position, to "get lucky" you must let the people making the decisions know that. Highly qualified candidates are often overlooked because the person making the decision didn't know they were interested. Throughout my business career I have seen this happen too many times to mention. People either don't ask for consideration or don't prepare themselves for the job they desire.

You might see that dream job in your present company.

Some people only think about all the reasons they can never attain it. Others look at a dream job as a long-term goal they can accomplish with much hard work. It's true that there are usually many steps between you and your dream job. But it will be preparation—not luck—that will make the difference. To be "lucky," you will have to work diligently on each step, not taking any shortcuts. Tell the people in charge about the job that interests you and ask them what you must do to qualify. If this job doesn't come your way the first time, don't be discouraged—just work harder.

Getting lucky isn't as easy as it looks. Be persistent in everything you do. If your career is not moving as fast as you would like, make an appointment with the boss to discuss how you can move up to where you want to be. Keep up the good work and luck will come your way.

As we all know, the job market is subject to change. The only security you have is your ability to perform. We hear bad news daily. There will be two hundred people laid off. Who will lose their job? This is a tough decision for a boss. When the layoffs are done, the boss has to do the same work with fewer people. The "lucky" ones left will be the ones that showed up at work every day on time. The "lucky" ones are the people who were always there at night when extra help was needed. The "lucky" ones never gave the boss a hard time over trivial matters. Again I ask, "Why are some people so lucky?"

I once read about this lady who bought a scratch ticket and won a million dollars, to be paid out fifty grand per year for twenty years. Now, on the surface she would have to be considered very lucky. What I did not tell you is that this same person spends twice that much per year on scratch tickets. What we have here is not a lucky lady but someone with a severe gambling addiction. I have personally found out through my own work life that the harder I work, the luckier I get.

To Recap:

- Most lucky people work very hard
- Preparation and assertiveness will make you lucky
- The best employees (the lucky ones) are not the first to be laid off
- The harder you work the luckier you get

Chapter 20
Maintain Loyalty

Loyalty within a company is important to your success. Say you have been hired by XYZ Company and they are paying you a certain wage to perform a job. This company deserves your loyalty. But loyalty goes much beyond that. It shows others how much you appreciate the opportunity given to you. Allow me to explain further. . . .

Never speak badly of the business that is providing for you and your family. It is so easy to complain about the little stuff that goes wrong. There might be some very nasty people within the company—one may even be your boss—however, that does not give you the right to be disloyal. My best advice is that you give 100 percent effort and be very positive when talking about your company. As long as you are in their employ, they deserve your trust. Your boss and coworkers also deserve your allegiance. I know this is a two-way street, but loyalty must begin with you.

I can remember once getting a call from an old customer who needed a favor. When he was a customer of mine, he was extremely loyal and a great friend. His first words to me were that he could no longer be of help to me and would understand if I couldn't help him with this particular favor. My answer to him was that I could never forget how wonderful he was to me in the past. This man gave me more business over a twenty-year period than just about any other person I can think of. Then I told him that I would consider it a privilege to do him this favor.

Be Loyal to Your Boss

Remember, your boss has a tough task trying to do his job and at the same time keep everyone happy. Be loyal to your boss simply because he or she is your boss. Look for ways to make his or her job easier. The boss needs your loyalty to do his or her job well. When people turn on the boss and do not support him or her, it makes for a difficult work environment. If there is a big problem that people are having with the boss's style of management, you or someone else should first try to discuss it directly with him or her. This works better than undermining what the boss is trying to accomplish.

One of my bosses was extremely loyal and went out of her way for me on many occasions. When I lost some business, she was very understanding and knew that I did everything possible to keep it. There was never any animosity toward me because she trusted that I would make it up somewhere else. I also never put her on the spot. If for whatever reason I had to leave my territory driving the company car, I would let her know ahead of time. The reason for this was simple. Should I be involved in an accident while being out of my area, she would know where I was and wouldn't feel like she was ambushed. We had this relationship of blind loyalty that was unusual, to say the least. If someone calls you a "loyal friend," wear it as a badge of honor. There is no higher compliment one person can pay another.

Be Loyal to Your Customers

Smart companies that want to stay in business realize they must be loyal to their customers. You can never take a person's business for granted. Depending on a customer's level of commitment, you should let them know that their business is important, and continue to look for better ways to serve them. If this is a big account, a personal visit to their headquarters might be in order. A company that does this successfully will retain many more clients than they lose.

Be Loyal to Your Employees

What is the most valuable resource a company has? It is their employees. Offering a fair salary or hourly wage is a good place for them to start showing their appreciation. Giving great health insurance is probably the single best benefit you can give to your employees. Although pension plans are not being offered by many companies, it surely helps in recruiting new employees. As previously mentioned, some companies offer their employees tax-free savings plans for retirement in the form of a 401(k). Yearly bonuses for exceeding goals are also a great incentive. These are major ways in which a company can show loyalty to their employees.

The boss can award a number of little gratuities for a job that is well done. For example, a gift certificate (even for twenty-five dollars) to each member of a team for their weekly teamwork is always appreciated. Writing a letter of appreciation to the people involved in a successfully completed project means a great deal to everyone involved. Holiday parties are nice, but unexpected acts of kindness go a long way in showing loyalty to employees.

A successful business shares the wealth and takes care of their people. Such companies will be rewarded by their workers' continued loyalty.

To Recap:

- Loyalty within a company is important to your success
- Never speak badly of the people who are paying you
- If someone calls you a "loyal friend," wear it as a badge of honor
- The business of a customer should never be taken for granted
- Companies must also be loyal to their employees

Chapter 21

Plan for Success

Your ultimate job might be the CEO of a Fortune 500 company, but it's the daily achievement of meaningful goals that gives you the best start. Plan to be successful. Expect to work extra hours and more days than most. Total commitment along with great social skills will give you the best chance to navigate through the ranks of upper management. Timing and being prepared are crucial. There is only one CEO. However, there are plenty of great jobs near the top.

Most new employees know what is necessary to succeed in their job. The responsibilities are usually well-defined. Exceed your given goals and you will have some job security. Always do more than expected in every task that you undertake. Be helpful to everyone you work with and enthusiastically support them.

The decisions you make on a daily basis are important to your success. Think about how they affect you and your coworkers. In the final analysis one must consider what is best for the company.

Don't Forget to Ask!

Success is there for the asking yet people don't see it. A great example of this was my largest customer. After working on this account for four years, I still had nothing to show for it. A number of promises were made, but the doctor in charge never gave me any business. In fact, this account belonged to my competitor for many years prior to my hire.

The chief of pediatrics had a very close relationship with the other company; and when push came to shove, I didn't accomplish anything. Finally this chief retired and a new one was hired. Needless to say, my not having any business at his hospital wouldn't make the list of items that he would be concerned about. I thought long and hard about whether I should make an appointment with him right away. Maybe I should wait a month or two. Since I had no business to lose, I decided to make an appointment.

When I went to see him, I was prepared with all my facts. He just sat and listened as I told him about all that I had done for the hospital and the many promises made to me (that I would obtain some business). After I completed presenting my case, he made a couple of telephone calls to verify my facts. When he got off the phone, he asked me how long it would take for me to start. I told him that my products could be shipped in overnight and I would be ready in the morning to service his account. I knew this would not be easy. Getting this done before the competition knew about what had transpired was most important. He told me that as of tomorrow morning the business would be mine.

What I didn't realize when I decided to ask for the business was that this gave him the opportunity to let people know he was the new boss. The moral of this story is simple. Don't forget to ask for the business. No one will give it to you without your asking.

Give a Little Extra

Some people who are starting their first job are not thinking about success and goals. This will come later, when they figure out what they really want to do for rest of their life. Regardless of what other people are (not) doing, to keep your current job it's very important to make the extra effort that will set you apart from the rest. Again, this means getting to work a little early, staying a little late, helping your coworkers when they need it, volunteering for extra projects, being cross-trained for other jobs, and doing whatever else is necessary to stand out among your peers.

Many people don't think about the consequences of their actions. This makes it easier for the people that do. Always do what you know in your heart is right. There are no secrets to success. It takes a tremendous amount of hard work, and many people are not willing to do it. In the workplace of today, you have to be productive in order to survive. It doesn't matter what school you went to. Your boss wants to know that you are contributing to the success of the company. Those who contribute will be rewarded with raises, bonuses, promotions, and job security.

To Recap:

- Total commitment is necessary to climb the corporate ladder
- One must do more than what is expected in this work environment to achieve some level of job security
- The order will not be yours until you ask for the business
- Make the extra effort that will set you apart from the rest
- Always do what is right
- You must be productive to survive

Chapter 22

Learn by Listening

If it wasn't for a baby's listening skills, he or she would never learn to speak. The better your listening skills as an adult, the smarter you will become. You can talk for twenty-four hours straight and not learn a thing. Conversely, if you listen intently for thirty minutes, you can learn a great deal. Most successful people are great listeners.

Becoming a good listener was not easy for me. I was always in too much of a hurry to make my point. When someone was talking, I would start formulating my response and usually stop listening halfway through the conversation. Has this ever happened to you? If it has, think about ways in which you can improve your listening skills. You must be conscious of the problem before you can address it.

After reading some books about successful people, I realized that they were all great listeners. I made a conscious effort to change. When someone talks to me now, they have my undivided attention. It is not that I am being kind and respectful to them, which I am, but that I am learning something. At the end of our conversation, I make sure that both of us have a mutual understanding of the facts.

As a new employee, listening skills very well determine how long you will be around. When you are meeting with the boss or listening to someone speaking at a meeting, you have to train yourself to pay close attention. First, you must maintain good eye contact. This is a person's first clue that you are listening. Then you must keep an open mind and try not to guess where the conversation is going. If you do guess, you might stop actively listening and lose the rest of what is being said. Don't try to prepare your response before a person finishes talking. You could be completely off track, and then they'll know you weren't listening. If this happens to you once, apologize. Explain that you were a little preoccupied. Ask this person to go over it again, and you best be hanging on their every word.

If you make a habit of not listening, your job will be in jeopardy. What you should also do is smile and nod, where appropriate, when the boss is speaking. Take notes concerning the main idea and ask questions at the end to make sure you understand. This will ensure that you are doing exactly what the boss wants and, thus, stay in his or her good graces. This is not only a good work idea but will help in your personal life. Much of what we learn is the result of good listening.

Think about everything that you negotiate in a given month. When you buy a car, listen intently—inattentiveness can cost you hundreds of dollars (or more). When the dealer tells you your finance rate, the cost of all the extras, the dealer prep, and anything else, you had better write it all down. Too often the cost that you were promised is not what you end up signing for. The same can be said about hiring a lawn service, buying an appliance, or applying for a mortgage. People often promise you the moon and deliver less. The reason this happens is that many customers are not good listeners. A person like you, who is a great listener, will truly get the great deal. This skill can save you thousands of dollars over the course of a lifetime and make you a much more valuable employee.

To Recap:

- You must listen to become smart
- How well you listen may determine how long you will be employed
- Whatever you negotiate to buy will cost you more if you don't listen carefully (car, house, etc.)
- Good listeners are valuable employees

Chapter 23

Speak the Truth

When you have a reputation for being truthful in the workplace, people place a great deal of value on what you say. When you think about the number of people that you deal with on a continuing basis, it makes sense that you always tell the truth. If you are caught in a lie, your credibility is gone.

Being truthful at all times in business today is very difficult. We are in such a competitive environment and every negative action or accusation could be very costly. You are better off losing a sale or admitting to a mistake and maintaining your credibility. There will be other sales opportunities, but being caught in a lie is a relationship breaker. Nobody wants to do business with someone they can't trust.

Sales people have gotten a bad reputation over the years when it comes to telling the truth. However, I know that the best sales people do just that. I sold for thirty-seven years, and the people I dealt with always trusted me. They knew that I could be taken at my word. This was instrumental to my success.

Everyone I know in business is in sales to a certain degree. No matter what your job is, you must be credible to be accepted by your coworkers and boss. You also must sell your ideas. Some people are very skilled, while others work hard to make their case. Whether you are on the phone, at a meeting, or selling on the road, always telling the truth is important. At the same time, you must be enthusiastic about what you are doing. If you are not energized about what you are saying, I can assure you that the person listening won't be excited either.

Don't exaggerate the benefits of what you are selling. People sometimes overstate the value. Don't tell someone that your product will last twenty years when you can't back it up. You might have the best product on the market, but that comment could kill the sale. Sell the features that have the most value so that you can tailor them to the needs of the customer. For example, be truthful about your higher purchase price, but then talk about quality, timely shipping, superior service, and anything else that you can offer as an advantage. Truth is a powerful weapon that can be used to your benefit.

One elderly salesman came up to me when I first started. He asked me how the job was going. I told him that work was going well but I had much to learn. At that point he asked, "Would you like some advice?" To which I replied, "I would love some." He informed me that never lying to a customer means never having to remember what was said. I took this to heart and always followed his advice.

At the same time, you must be careful when it comes to being truthful with your fellow employees. You don't want to suggest changes to "fix" the people you work with. You may think they badly need a shave or haircut. Their wardrobe might not be to your liking and their work habits could be terrible. Expressing these opinions will alienate you from your coworkers. Unless you are the boss, respect their right to be different, and don't mention anything. You want to be known as the person who everyone can believe in and depend on when they need help. Always be truthful, and this will make you stand out among your coworkers.

To Recap:

- When you have a reputation for being truthful, people place a great deal of value on what you say
- Lie to a person once and forever lose your credibility
- Never lying is never having to remember what you said
- Telling the truth is always your best option

Chapter 24
Avoid Problems

I'm not going to talk about the obvious "not to dos" here, like being late, leaving early, and fighting with the boss. I want to take this time to discuss some issues you might not have thought about. One simple way of looking at "what not to do" is to think about whether the boss would be happy about what you are doing.

Slow Down, Then Make an Informed Decision

The best advice I can give you is to think long and hard before making any important decisions at work. Take all the time you need to make the most informed choice possible. Sometimes just by sleeping on a decision and waiting until the next day to communicate (or enact) it will put a new perspective on your available options.

Keep Work Relationships Professional

Today, more than ever, you work closely with people for long hours and this can lead to trusting friendships. At the same time, this might lead to more than just being friends. Office romances, like many relationships, usually don't work out for the long term. Avoid them. When relationships end, often one (or both) of the people involved is not happy about it. Now you have to work with this person eight to ten hours a day, every day. What used to be a great work environment is now a nightmare. If you feel that a person you work with is very special and you want to pursue a relationship, obtain a transfer to another department first. If that is not possible, at least think about some other options that might solve your problem.

Never borrow money from a coworker! You might

not be able to pay them back as promised. If this is the case, find the money somewhere to pay back money owed. Should you not be able to repay a debt, word will spread rapidly throughout the office. You will quickly get a tarnished reputation at work and this will be detrimental to your future career.

The same can be said about lending money. If a coworker asks for money, simply say you don't have any extra to lend, but you will be more than happy to buy lunch. If you lend out cash and the coworker is then unable to repay, a once great friendship will become a strained one. That is why you must think before you act.

Also, don't assume that what you see makes it fact. Just because someone is not wearing a wedding ring doesn't mean they are single. Don't swear or tell off-color jokes. Your audience might not think they are funny and may find them offensive. People have been fired for less. Be very careful about what you say. Everyone is judgmental to various degrees and has strong opinions. Don't bring up a controversial subject unless you are willing to live with the possible consequences. All such actions could become career killers.

Now, you might have a mild-mannered boss. When talking to him, always stay away from saying anything that might be considered controversial. Let's say you are conversing with him about pets. Don't tell him that all pit bulls are vicious and should be outlawed. He might be married with three kids and own a pit bull. He may not even tell you that he has one, but he will not forget what you said. When you don't realize that you screwed up, you can't even do damage control.

One other point worth mentioning is socializing with your work associates. It is very common for coworkers to go out on Thursday or Friday night after work for a couple of drinks. You don't have to go every week, but showing up one out of three might be a good idea. When you do go, I strongly advise you sip a few drinks and be a good listener. Save the partying for later with your personal friends. This is also a good opportunity to meet people who might work in other departments.

If one of your coworkers goes on a tirade about a person in the office, keep your mouth shut. If you don't have anything good to say about someone, say nothing at all. On the other hand, when they compliment someone you know and like, jump in and agree. You also don't want to be the last to leave. When people start departing, make your exit. The last one to leave is usually considered the party guy or gal. And it's safe to assume that what happens that night finds its way back to the office. When the boss is looking to promote someone, it won't be the party guy or gal, or will it? You constantly have to think. Your boss might be a party guy or a nondrinker or somewhere in between. Again, these are important questions that you must have the answers to. You can never have enough information. Knowledge is power. When in doubt, don't do it or don't say it.

To Recap:

- Think long and hard before making any important decisions at work (maybe sleep on it)
- Office romances are not a good idea
- Don't borrow or lend money at work (work can become very uncomfortable if payback is not made)
- Be sociable yet professional with your coworkers (party hardy later with your friends)
- When in doubt, don't do it or don't say it
- Knowledge is power

Chapter 25
When All Else Fails

There will be a time in your career when you feel the sky is falling and nothing is going right. It might be the major project you were in charge of failed. Whatever the case, this is a great time to sit down and think about your options. You still have a job and you don't want to lose it. This is a great time to be seen and not heard. Don't offer constructive criticism about anything. Your boss could construe the criticism as negativity, which will be one more factor working against you. This is a great time to devote all your energy to the job. If anyone notices the difference, just tell that person you're on a deadline. Don't work hard for a week and stop. Now is the perfect time to rediscover yourself. The people around you must be convinced of your sincerity.

Don't ask for favors when your job might be in jeopardy. Forget about asking to leave early for a ball game. Maybe you were hoping to take a Friday afternoon off to start your weekend trip. Don't do it. You want your boss to see you working longer hours, assisting everyone in the office, volunteering where needed, and doing whatever it takes to make his or her life easier.

Sometimes you are a victim, being singled out by the boss, when you know it's unjust. If this happens, make an appointment with the boss and plead your case. Never, and I mean never, bring it up in front of others. At this point your boss is going to give you reasons why he or she is displeased, and more than likely won't change his or her mind. Leave that meeting on a positive note. You can say, "I'm sorry you feel that way, but I can assure you that I will do everything necessary to regain your trust."

Some people will leave that meeting and sulk. There will be a number of willing participants in the office for a pity party. If you decide to go this route, you are on your way out of a job. Nobody said life was fair. You must commit yourself to excellence and forget about the unfairness done to you. This situation comes up constantly, and most of the time this difference of opinion isn't personal. We often take it as such because we are hurt and think that our job could be in jeopardy. You are probably one of many people your boss is having an issue with. Handle it properly and all will be well. In two weeks this whole incident will be forgotten, and the office will be dealing with a new set of issues.

It is never as bad as it seems, and how you react to mere disagreement makes all the difference. Do as I suggest, and in six months your job will be secure once again.

To Recap:

- When you experience failure, work harder and complain about nothing
- Don't ask for favors when your job is in jeopardy
- If singled out by the boss, try to privately meet and work the issue out
- Commit yourself to excellence and you will ride out the bad times

Chapter 26

Seize the Moment

At times you will be the star of the month, the quarter, or even the year. This is when you have bargaining power and should ask for the moon. However, your leverage is limited, so think about what is important to you at this time. It might be money. Obviously, being number one in the office will merit you a raise, but how much? This is the time to sit down with the boss and make your case. If you know that 5 percent is a good raise, ask for 10 percent. You might receive it. If you don't ask, there is no chance. The boss may tell you that there isn't enough money in the budget, but will give you 8 percent. You are still ahead of the game.

This is also a great time to ask for a promotion. Make sure that you communicate all the reasons you deserve the new position and why you are qualified. For some people the extra money or the promotion is not important. They are excellent employees who consider their family to be top priority. This is also the time to negotiate a better work situation. Your baby is in daycare and you would like to work two days from home. If that's what you want, you must be able to show the boss how you can do this without disrupting the office. You might start by saying that you will be flexible with your days, so as to not miss important meetings. Assure your boss that, when at home, you will work late into the night, if necessary, to make sure the work is done. You might get your two days, or maybe one. Being the best employee gives you some power. Your boss wants to keep you happy. Your boss doesn't want to tell his or her own supervisor that the best employee has left the company.

I can remember getting a new boss many years ago. The word on the street was that he was tough and you had to be prepared when he worked with you. At this time I was the top salesman in the district, so I knew I had some leverage. On the first day we met, he didn't want to start with coffee. I remember him saying, "Let's go to work."

Not much was said that day, but he took copious notes. At 5:00 p.m. I was taking him back to his car because I had a monthly pediatric dinner to attend that would not finish until 9:30 p.m. At this point he stated to me: "If you are going to a pediatric dinner tonight, so am I."

We went to the dinner and didn't return to his car until 10:00 p.m. I told him to be careful driving home. He then announced that we had to evaluate my day's work. This we did for another hour. When done, he wanted to know if I had any questions. I asked him if we could talk man to man, off the record. To this he replied, absolutely. I then asked him, "Do you want the best out of Mike Bradley?" He assured me that he did. Then I told him, "I understand you're the boss, and I will do whatever you say. However, if you want the best out of Mike Bradley, you will leave me alone."

There was an eerie silence. He then told me he would take this under advisement. I can't give you a good reason why I said it. This was very much out of character for me. I guess that was the way I felt at the time and I spoke my mind. This is not something I would recommend anyone do. Once these words left my lips, I couldn't take them back. However, I was very sincere and not threatening. Being top salesman in his group didn't hurt either.

I went home and told my wife what I did and that I would probably be fired. But, being a smart boss, who knew how to manage each person differently, he decided to leave me alone, and never worked with me again during his tenure. Needless to say, I never mentioned any of this to my coworkers. I also did my part by staying at or near the top. If I were to falter, he would have been on my case. The only reason this worked was that I had a great reputation for working very hard and getting results.

Now, you might not be the star in the office, but perhaps you're having a great year. This is also the time for you to ask for favors. Again, think about what is important to you and go for it. When you are one of the top guns, the boss will usually give you his undivided attention.

Timing is crucial. Don't ask for favors when all is not going well in the office. Wait for the right moment when your boss is in a great mood and has a chance to talk. Also, pick the time of the day when activity is a little less hectic.

There are many people who think they should be rewarded for doing an exemplary job. Let's say you are the boss of three great employees. There are only so many promotions and a limited raise pool. Two employees come to you and make a case for big raises and promotions. The third doesn't come to you at all. You might feel that the third employee is happy with his present position and yearly raise; therefore, that third person will probably be slighted. You don't want to be that third person.

Top athletes have agents who spend their entire careers thinking of every possible reason why their athletes deserve more money, more perks, and more years on their contract. Be a great agent for yourself and do the same. Now is the time to seize the moment.

Exercise:

Sit down with a piece of paper and write three things that are important to you, along with a reason why you deserve each one.

To Recap:

- When on top, ask for the moon
- Top performers have earned the right to ask for a promotion or more money
- The best employees can negotiate better working arrangements
- Be a great agent for yourself or you may be slighted
- You must seize the moment

Chapter 27

Understand the Differences

Within any organization your very existence depends on how you relate to the people you work with. That is why it is most important for you to take into consideration the age, tenure, personality type, and temperament of your supervisors.

Say your boss is twenty-seven years old. (This is more of the norm today.) You know right away that he is on a fast track. This type of person will likely be open to new ideas that will make him stand out. He will be more likely to take chances. So do not hesitate to offer him a suggestion that has never been tried before. But then you have to consider his personality type. If he is the analytical type, you better be able to explain all the facts and figures and where they come from. If he is the happy-go-lucky, amiable type, you might be able to talk in generalities. He will worry about the details later.

On the other hand, let's say your boss is fifty-nine years old and has been working at the company for thirty years. My guess is that she is zeroed in on retirement and will do nothing to jeopardize that. You better be very well versed in the company rules and follow them to a tee. Don't buck the system and try to change protocols in the office. This boss probably believes in a strong work ethic in order to last so long. Come in early and stay late. Volunteer to help with special projects and company functions. Odds are good that such a company person would appreciate that. If you have a great idea that is outside the box, you might want to suggest that a team of people, including the boss, weigh all the options and make the final decision. With an approach like this, you have a better chance of getting new projects approved.

When I talk about the "young boss" and the "old boss," I'm creating stereotypes. Before you do anything, take the time to find out exactly who you are dealing with. We all are amateur psychologists. Obviously, some are better than others. If you have the gift of being able to read people, it's a great asset in the workplace. If you don't, you are going to have to find a friend you can trust who does.

You also must think about the different personalities and habits that your coworkers possess. To succeed at your job, you must understand these differences.

Don't ever put a coworker in an awkward situation. For example, their financial situation could be much different than yours. If you are working on a project with this person and they bring their lunch daily, you might want to do the same. Don't talk to them about the big vacation you are planning. Talk about your kids or the local sports team or anything else you might have in common. Try to build some sort of bond with everyone you work with. We are all unique. Remember that knowledge is power and this is a great example of that. When you know how someone is different from you, it enables you to relate to that person on a level that he or she will understand.

If you haven't done so yet, sit down with a piece of paper and analyze all of the people you work with and for. It will be an eye-opening exercise for you. Some people are on autopilot and treat everyone the same, which is not a good idea. Understanding the differences among people is instrumental to your success. This is also a good exercise to complete a month into any new job.

To Recap:

- Your mere existence depends on how well you relate to fellow coworkers
- The age and personality type of your boss might determine how to best relate to him or her
- Don't ever place a coworker in an awkward situation (e.g., discussing your fancy vacation with a coworker who is having financial problems)
- Understanding the differences among people is instrumental to your success

Chapter 28

Build a Solid Foundation

The job environment has changed so much over the years. Past generations took a job and held it for forty years. We are in a much different marketplace today, and the chances of keeping the same job for a long time are less likely. Remember, the only security you have at a company today is the space between your ears. So you better think of ways to make yourself vital to the company.

I have tried to open up your mind and help you deal with the many problems people face in the workplace. Most of what I told you has been experienced by me during my career. The decisions you make every day could affect you for the rest of your life. If you go on autopilot, you are sure to have a rocky ride and probably crash. Let's review some of the important steps you should take in order to keep your job.

- Do the easy stuff: smile, laugh aloud, dress smart, be prompt, and make as many friends in the workplace as possible.
- New employees should keep a low profile. Set reasonable goals, volunteer to help at company events, be the go-to guy or gal, and stay away from office politics.
- Take advantage of company-offered courses and tuition reimbursement programs. Become cross-trained in a number of areas for job security.
- Be organized and set up a daily schedule. Keep notes on your progress.
- Prepare for your meetings with the boss. Don't ever assume anything.
- If you want a raise or promotion, ask for it.

- Lead by example. When you have a problem, work to solve it.
- Enthusiastically support your coworkers. Be persistent in all that you do. The power of positive thinking cannot be overrated.
- Be loyal to your company, your boss, and all of your coworkers. Success is an adventure. No one said it would be easy, but it is a trip worth taking.
- Be a great listener. Listening intently is also a sign of respect. Speaking of respect, everyone deserves it.
- Seize the moment. Timing is everything. When the time is right, go for it.

At this point I would like to think that you understand we are in a people business. It is your people skills that will make you successful in the workplace. Do what is important for the success of the company, and maybe the job will be yours for as long as you want it.

To Recap:

- The only security you have at a company today is the space between your ears
- The daily decisions you make affect the rest of your life
- New employees should maintain a low profile
- Take advantage of company-offered courses and tuition reimbursement programs
- Prepare for your meetings and expect results
- Lead by example
- The power of positive thinking cannot be overrated
- Be a great listener
- When on top, seize the moment (ask for the moon)
- Your people skills are the key to your success in the workplace

Acknowledgments

Ira Smolowitz, PhD—I would like to give special thanks to Dr. Smolowitz for taking time out of his busy schedule to read my book and offer suggestions on how I might improve it. I did make some changes based on his evaluation.

Bernard Davidow—Bernie is a dear friend who has a fantastic grasp of the English language. I used and abused his talents to make my book much more readable. Thanks again for your words of wisdom.

Harry Weinmann—Harry is another good friend who took the time to read my book and offer some advice, which I did include. His help was very much appreciated.

Mike Valentino—Mike was very helpful in the final edit of this book.

About the Author

Michael Bradley successfully navigated the minefields of the workplace at Bristol-Myers Squibb Co., Inc. for a period of thirty-seven years. The most amazing aspect of this story is that he accomplished this while doing the same job, by choice, under a number of different supervisors, for all these years.

During his tenure Mike won every major award the company had to offer for sales excellence. Among the honors bestowed on him was the famed "Legend Award" that, to this day, has only been presented to a select few. This tribute is given in recognition of many years of dedicated, loyal service and an outstanding record of consistently superior sales performance. The day Mike retired from his many years of service, his sales ranking was number one in the country out of some four hundred-fifty employees. He will tell you that having a great work ethic played a major role in his success.

Being married and having three girls was reason enough for Mike to wake up early every morning and go to work with a sense of purpose. His family depended on his tenacity, and he was not about to disappoint those who loved him so dearly.

For more information, please visit:
www.jobsecurity.biz

CPSIA information can be obtained at www.ICGtesting.com
Printed in the USA
BVOW010023240712

295969BV00007B/1/P

9 781938 690020